"*Opposites Attract*"

"Opposites Attract"
Four One Act Comedies

Bruce Kane

Writers Club Press
San Jose New York Lincoln Shanghai

"Opposites Attract"
Four One Act Comedies

Writers Club Press
an imprint of iUniverse.com, Inc.

For information address:
iUniverse.com, Inc.
5220 S 16th, Ste. 200
Lincoln, NE 68512
www.iuniverse.com

ISBN: 0-595-14893-X

"Opposites Attract"

SETTING: Sometimes a bar, sometimes not a bar.

TIME: Now.

(The lights come up on three empty stools. BETTY, a Valley housewife enters and addresses the audience.)

BETTY	Hi. My name is Betty Corbin. I'm thirty eight years old. I'm trying to lose eight pounds. (She sits on an end stool. A conservatively dressed man enters. He introduces himself to the audience)
DAVE	I'm Dave Corbin. I'm thirty nine. Today my top spin forehand was devastating…I won six-three…Six-four. (He sits on the center stool. A sexy young woman enters and greets the audience)
SHELLEY	My name is Michelle. But everyone calls me Shelley. I'll be twenty eight next month. I still wear a size six. *(She sits on the third stool.)*
BETTY	I have a lovely home in the Valley. Five bedrooms, three and a half baths.
DAVE	My office is in Century City.
SHELLEY	I own a condo in what the real estate ladies like to refer to as Beverly Hills adjacent.

BETTY   I'm a housewife.

DAVE   I'm an attorney.

SHELLEY   I run my own interior design firm.

BETTY   I have two kids and a dog named Millie. She was
                 given to us by my Uncle Ned. He's a Republican.
                 Uncle Ned that is. Millie is a cocker spaniel.

SHELLEY   I've never been married.

DAVE   I drive an 89 BMW. It's my pride and joy.

BETTY   I've been married to the same man for fifteen years.

SHELLEY   I've been sleeping with the same man for eight months.

DAVE   I play tennis twice a month with Barbra Streisand's
                 lawyer.

BETTY   My husband is a wonderful man. He takes very good
                 care of me and the kids.

DAVE   They deserve it.

SHELLEY   My lover and I see each other whenever we can.

DAVE   Neither of us likes to be crowded.

BETTY   It's not the same as it was when Dave and I first got married. Then, he'd call me up in the middle of the day…right out of the blue…and tell me to wait for him in bed. I loved sex in the afternoon.

DAVE   I was in law school then. There was time.

BETTY   He doesn't come home in the afternoon anymore.

DAVE   Hell, it's forty five minutes from the office to the house alone. And that's if there's no traffic on the freeway.

SHELLEY   I sometimes think the only attraction I hold for Dave is the proximity of my apartment to his office. He can be in and out before anyone at the firm misses him.

DAVE   It goes much deeper than that. I love being with Shelley. She's bright…beautiful…independent… Never demanding…Last week I took her to Las Vegas with me for a lawyer's convention. Just the two of us for the whole week. It was great. We had a wonderful time.

SHELLEY   He did take me to Las Vegas for a week. He said we'd have all kinds of time to be alone. We were alone alright. He didn't want any of his pals to see us together.

BETTY   Dave works very hard. And we try to get away when we can. He really wanted me to go with him to Las Vegas last week. He had this lawyer's convention. He said we could turn the whole thing into a second honeymoon and it would all be tax deductible. I was looking forward to it…Then the kids got the flu and Dave had to go by himself.

DAVE   It would have been a second honeymoon. But just because Betty couldn't make it, I saw no reason why I should go alone.

SHELLEY   I hope it doesn't sound like I'm complaining. Dave and I have a very good relationship. We like each other. The sex is good and I'm not limited to just one man.

DAVE   I didn't know that…About not being limited.

BETTY   Don't think I'm not grateful for my life. It's hectic and we don't get as much time away from the kids as we'd like, but it's a good life.

SHELLEY   I have my independence.

BETTY   I have security.

SHELLEY   I have a great job.

BETTY   I have a wonderful home.

SHELLEY   I drive a red convertible.

BETTY   We paid off the station wagon last month.

SHELLEY   My apartment has a built in sauna.

BETTY   We've got our own pool.

SHELLEY   Dave says I'm the fulfillment of every erotic fantasy he's every had and he dresses me in garters, black seamed stockings and stiletto heels to prove it.

DAVE   A guy's gotta have some fantasy fulfillment.

SHELLEY   I don't mind....Really.

BETTY   Dave never fails to compliment me on my cooking. He says eating my lasagna is the closest thing to sex he's ever encountered.

DAVE   I'm not ashamed to admit it...I've got it all...A successful law practice...A beautiful home...Two terrific kids...A wife who never complains...And a girlfriend with legs like a Rockette...And an 89 BMW.

SHELLEY   Who would have ever believed it? Here I am at age twenty eight with everything I ever wanted…And I don't know where the hell I'm going.

BETTY   I'm right where I belong…Why do I feel like I haven't been anywhere?

DAVE   I couldn't be happier.

SHELLEY   The business, the bills, the clients, the suppliers, the phone…What does it all mean?

BETTY   The kids, the house, the car pool, the gardener, the PTA. My life isn't my own.

SHELLEY   I want a little security…Is that too much to ask?

BETTY   I want to be independent…Have a life of my own.

SHELLEY   I'm lonely.

BETTY   I'm bored.

SHELLEY   I want a home.

BETTY   I want adventure.

SHELLEY   I want children.

BETTY   I want freedom.

SHELLEY   I want to be loved.

BETTY   I want to thrill to the touch of new hands on my body.

SHELLEY   I want to wake up with the same man every morning.

BETTY   I want to drive a red convertible.

SHELLEY   I want a Volvo.

BETTY   I want to be some man's wet dream come to life.

DAVE   I want a serve like Pete Sampras.

SHELLEY   *(Turning to Dave)* I want to get married.

BETTY   *(Turning to Dave)* I want a divorce. *(Betty and Shelley change places)*

SHELLEY   My name is Shelley Corbin now.

BETTY   I thought about going back to my maiden name for a while...But Betty Selman doesn't exist anymore. She was somebody I knew a long time ago...In another life.

DAVE   Everyone seems to have adjusted to the new arrangement.

SHELLEY   I'm thirty years old now.

BETTY   I just experienced the big four oh.

DAVE   I'd rather not talk about it.

SHELLEY   Dave and I live in a small house in the Valley with his two kids. Dave is a very good husband. He works very hard to take care of us.

BETTY   I'm single...I live in a one bedroom apartment.

DAVE   I still practice law.

SHELLEY   I do some interior design work from time to time. Just to keep my hand in...I'm thinking of taking it up full time again...But, what with the kids and the house...

BETTY   I got a job...I'm a receptionist with a small insurance firm in Woodland Hills.

DAVE   I had to sell the BMW. Broke my heart.

BETTY   I bought a convertible. It's a Plymouth. It's old. An eighty something. It's in the shop now…I'm having it painted red.

SHELLEY   I drive car pool three days a week.

BETTY   I took a lover. We've been sleeping together for eight months now.

DAVE   I still play tennis with Barbra Streisand's lawyer twice a week.

SHELLEY   I'm trying to lose nine pounds.

BETTY   I miss my kids.

DAVE   The firm is growing…We're looking for office space in Santa Monica.

SHELLEY   I found these shoes Dave gave me before we were married. The ones right out of an S and M manual? One of the heels was broken…I didn't get it fixed.

BETTY   My lover just called.

SHELLEY   Look at the time...I'd better get home...The kids
                 must be getting hungry.

BETTY   He's coming over.

SHELLEY   Dave just phoned.

BETTY   He asked me to meet him in bed.

SHELLEY   He said he'd be a little late.

BETTY   He doesn't have much time...He has to get home.
                 (She hurries off excitedly)

SHELLEY   He asked me to hold dinner for him. *(She kind of
                 shrugs and walks off)*

DAVE   *(Starts to leave then turns back.)* Did I mention I sold
                 the BMW? I really miss that car. *(He exits past LOIS,
                 a well dressed woman sitting with MASON, a love
                 smitten man)*

LOIS   Of course, I love you Mason. You're kind and gentle.
                 You're steady...Reliable...Dependable...I know a life
                 with you would be steady....reliable...dependable.

MASON   I'd always look after you, Lois. You know that.

LOIS   You'd never give me reason to worry, would you?

MASON   I'd see to it that you never had a trouble in the world.

LOIS   I know that you're not the kind of man who'd ever cheat on me.

MASON   You have my solemn word.

LOIS   Robert was always leaving me alone.

MASON   I'd be with you night and day.

LOIS   Robert would be gone for days without telling where he was going.

MASON   I'd report to you hourly. You'd know where I was night and day.

LOIS   I never knew who he was with. Although I eventually learned about…the women.

MASON   You're the only woman I need, Lois.

LOIS   That's when he started sending me flowers…Every time he strayed he'd send me flowers…Endless bouquets of flowers. Peace offerings. *(The following list is spoken with rising emotions)* Mums, roses, carnations, lilies, birds of paradise, begonias, asters, impatiens, pansies...He filled every room in the house with them.

MASON   Appalling.

LOIS   *(Orgasmic)* The scent was intoxicating.

(You don't have to drop a building on Mason, who gets up and exits past a sexy, distant woman sitting alone, perhaps smoking a cigarette. TED enters. He sees the woman...Slowly he begins to circle her, eyeing her from head to toe and everywhere in between. Finally, he speaks...)

TED   I love you.

BARBARA   What?

TED   I love you.

BARBARA   Are you talking to me?

TED   Yes...I love you.

BARBARA   You don't even know me.

TED   That's why I love you.

BARBARA   If you'll excuse me.

TED   I've been looking for you all my life.

BARBARA   I've heard that line before.

TED   I mean it. You're perfect. Your nose is perfect. You
               hair is perfect. Your lips are perfect. Your legs are per-
               fect. And...Your breasts are perfect.

BARBARA   I'm going to order lunch now.

TED   I need you.

BARBARA   I have no need to be needed.

TED   Perfect. I need a woman who has no need to be needed.

BARBARA   Well I don't need a man who needs a woman who has
               no need to be needed.

TED   I want you.

BARBARA   I'm unobtainable.

TED   That's why I want you.

BARBARA   I beg your pardon.

TED   I only want women I can't have. They never disappoint me.

BARBARA   That must make for long lasting relationships.

TED   Sarcasm in a woman turns me on.

BARBARA   We'd never get along.

TED   Is there someone else?

BARBARA   No.

TED   Are you emotionally involved?

BARBARA   I never get emotionally involved.

TED   Marry me.

BARBARA   I could never marry a man who actually wanted me.

TED   Of course.

BARBARA   A man who wanted me would also need me.

TED　　　　　I need you.

BARBARA　　　I know. That's why you can't have me.

TED　　　　　Have you ever been in love?

BARBARA　　　Hundreds of times.

TED　　　　　What happened?

BARBARA　　　They didn't know I was alive. It was wonderful. Have you ever been married?

TED　　　　　No. Cameron Diaz wouldn't return my calls. If I told you I didn't need you, didn't want you and didn't love you, what would you do?

BARBARA　　　Throw myself at your knees.

TED　　　　　I don't need you, I don't want you and I don't love you.

BARBARA　　　If only I could believe that.

TED　　　　　You hold no appeal for me at all.

BARBARA　　　Please stop.

TED   There are thousands of other women I'd rather be
                    with. Millions…

BARBARA   I won't listen to your honeyed words.

TED   Kiss off, baby. *(She throws herself at his knees)*

BARBARA   I'm yours. *(He pulls her to her feet. They kiss. During the
                    kiss his eyes wander.)*

TED   Do you know that woman over there?

BARBARA   Which woman?

TED   The blonde with the perfect nose, perfect hair, per-
                    fect legs and perfect breasts.

BARBARA   Forget it. She has a husband and a lover.

TED   I want her.

BARBARA   You can't have her.

TED   I know. *(He starts to leave)*

BARBARA   I thought it was me you didn't want.

TED   I've lost interest.

BARBARA   You can't. I need you.

TED   You're stifling my growth as a person.

BARBARA   She won't give you the time of day.

TED   Thrilling, isn't it?

BARBARA   But I want you.

TED   My heart belongs to another.

BARBARA   How can you walk out on me like this? After all we meant to each other. Can you forget the way I ignored you? Resisted you? Treated you like dirt?

TED   It was great while it lasted, baby, but it's over.

BARBARA   Nobody kept you at arm's length like I did.

TED   Until she came along.

BARBARA   You're breaking my heart.

TED   It's the least I can do.

BARBARA   What does she have that I don't have?

TED   She's unobtainable.

BARBARA   Well, then...Go after her. See if I care. *(He leaves.
                       Barbara sits alone. After a beat or two, Ted returns)*

TED   Hi baby.

BARBARA   Oh, you're back.

TED   She told me to get lost. I nearly came in my pants.

BARBARA   I know I'm the only one for you.

TED   I'll never forget the way she looked right through me
                       like I was a windshield.

BARBARA   You don't throw away what we had so quickly.

TED   Baby, I'm back.

BARBARA   Get lost.

TED   What?

BARBARA   I said, get lost.

TED   Nice try.

BARBARA   I mean it.

TED   I get it. Turnabout is fair play.

BARBARA   Hit the bricks.

TED   You're turning me on.

BARBARA   Take off.

TED   But, I love you.

BARBARA   Tough.

TED   I need you.

BARBARA   Lotsaluck.

TED   I want you.

BARBARA   Sorry, pal. You don't satisfy my needs.

TED   Just tell me what you want and I'll withhold it.

BARBARA   I need to know where I stand with a man. I need to know that his indifference is sincere. That my wants and desires will always come second, if at all. That he expects everything from me and will give me nothing in return. That way I can feel confident that there is no hope for the relationship. That I'll always be free. It's only with a man who doesn't give a damn about me that I can be truly liberated.

TED   There's someone else, isn't there?

BARBARA   Yes, there's someone else.

TED   I'm hurt.

BARBARA   I know.

TED   Thank you.

BARBARA   I'm not totally void of feeling.

TED   Who is it? Who's this two timer you haven't been seeing behind my back.

BARBARA   *(Pointing)* Him.

TED   Him?

BARBARA   Him…The one with the cruel eyes.

TED   He treats women like garbage.

BARBARA   I know.

TED   He'll break your heart.

BARBARA   I'm counting on it.

TED   Then this is it?

BARBARA   This is it.

TED   Well, I gotta say one thing for you, baby. You didn't disappoint me.

BARBARA   Goodbyes are so liberating. *(They exit in opposite directions. One of them walks past Lois, who is now sitting with Zeke.)*

LOIS   Robert would never do the things I wanted to do.

ZEKE   I'd see to it we did only the things you wanted to do.

LOIS   I always wanted to see Tahiti.

ZEKE   We'll honeymoon in Tahiti.

LOIS   Instead we went to New Zealand because Robert has
                a sheep ranch there.

ZEKE   You name it and we'll do it.

LOIS   The Greek Isles.

ZEKE   I'll book a cruise.

LOIS   The closest we got was Kenya.

ZEKE   Better yet, I'll charter a yacht.

LOIS   Robert wanted to see elephants.

ZEKE   You draw up the list. I'll make the reservations.

LOIS   Robert never listened to me. He never listened to any-
                one. He always did what he damn well wanted to do.

ZEKE	Sounds like a selfish bastard, if you ask me.
LOIS	*(Pridefully)* Robert never took shit from anybody. *(Zeke exits with his tail between his legs, a dilemma made even worse when he passes Greg and Tanya who enter carrying drinks and laughing gaily.)*
GREG	How long have we known each other?
TANYA	I don't know…Three, four hours.
GREG	I feel I've known you all my life.
TANYA	Isn't that funny? I was just thinking the same thing.
GREG	There are some people you know all your life and…
TANYA	You never really know them.
GREG	Exactly.
TANYA	My first husband was like that.
GREG	I knew it.
TANYA	Knew what?

GREG   That you'd been married before.

TANYA   You did? How?

GREG   I just knew.

TANYA   You're divorced, aren't you?

GREG   Two years.

TANYA   I knew it the first time I saw you.

GREG   Talk about simpatico.

TANYA   Was your first wife communicative?

GREG   Silent as a tomb.

TANYA   My ex was the same way.

GREG   That's why the marriage failed.

TANYA   To be honest, I wasn't a very open person myself.

GREG   I never would have guessed.

TANYA   It was only through therapy…

GREG   That you learned to say what you felt.

TANYA   You too?

GREG   Me too.

TANYA   Somehow I knew that.

GREG   I went into therapy a tightly closed bud and emerged an open flower reaching for the light.

TANYA   That's beautiful.

GREG   I've come to learn that only through complete and open communication can two people have any hope for a deep and lasting relationship.

TANYA   As long as that communication isn't one sided.

GREG   Both people must be able to freely express their thoughts, their needs, their desires…

TANYA   But it must be an honest expression of those needs and desires. No game playing.

GREG   You're a find, if you don't mind my saying so.

TANYA   Not at all.

GREG   Since my divorce, I've dated many women. They seem so protective.

TANYA   Defensive...

GREG   Afraid to say what they want.

TANYA   What they need. It's the same with men.

GREG   I don't mean to sound presumptuous, but I think you and have...

TANYA   A real future together?

GREG   You took the words right out of my mouth.

TANYA   You're an open book.

GREG   Coming from someone as forthright as yourself, that's a real compliment. The truth is I'm not as open as I'd like to be.

TANYA   I feel complimented that you can reveal that to me.

GREG   You see…I want to…

TANYA   The answer is yes.

GREG   But I haven't even asked the question.

TANYA   You want to have sex with me.

GREG   When it comes to open lines of communication, you could write the book.

TANYA   Don't be silly, I was thinking the same thing.

GREG   Actually, I've been thinking it…

TANYA   Since you bought me that second martini.

GREG   My God, are we on the same wave length or what?

TANYA   It's nothing magical really. We're just two open people who refuse to beat around the bush.

GREG   I could kiss you.

TANYA   Why don't you?

GREG   Exactly…Why don't I? *(They kiss)*

GREG   I don't know why I was so afraid to even broach the
              subject of sex. I knew you were going to say "yes."
              *(Tanya looks up slowly. Her whole demeanor changes
              from rosy openness to testy and defensive)*

TANYA   You did?

GREG   There was no question about it? This is amazing.

TANYA   Yes…Isn't it?

GREG   Oh, I'm never going to let you go.

TANYA   You knew I was going to say "yes"?

GREG   Absolutely.

TANYA   I could've said "no."

GREG   Not a chance. Waiter…Another martini for the lady.
              No olive this time.

TANYA   How did you know I..?

GREG   Didn't want an olive?

TANYA	I see…The same way you knew I'd say…
GREG	We have something very special here. There is nothing I would not be afraid to tell you. There are things I want to tell you. That I'm dying to tell you. Things I've never told anyone in my entire life.
TANYA	You knew I'd say "yes"?
GREG	This relationship cannot fail.
TANYA	Would you have been less interested if I had said "no"?
GREG	But you didn't. That's what makes it so perfect. You said "yes." I knew you were going to say "yes." You knew I was going to ask. I knew, you knew, I was going to ask.
TANYA	I've said "no" before.
GREG	I even know how you like to make love.
TANYA	Oh, you do, do you?
GREG	I know what your deepest unfulfilled romantic fantasy is.

TANYA   Really? And just what is my deepest unfulfilled
             romantic fantasy.

GREG   You want me to spell it out, right here?

TANYA   That's exactly what I want.

GREG   Courage thy name is woman. First of all, the setting.
             A room lit only by candles.

TANYA   Neon lights.

GREG   Uh uh…Candles.

TANYA   *Red* neon lights.

GREG   You're dressed in a negligee that's all silk and lace.

TANYA   Leather…Black leather…With studs.

GREG   There's music playing.

TANYA   What kind?

GREG   Soft music.

TANYA	Loud. Very loud.
GREG	Ravel's "Bolero."
TANYA	The Beatles' "Let's Do It In The Road."
GREG	I slowly and tantalizingly slide the straps of your negligee down your shoulders and gently kiss your neck.
TANYA	You bite it.
GREG	Your negligee falls to the floor.
TANYA	You rip it from my back.
GREG	I pick you up in my arms.
TANYA	You grab me by the hair.
GREG	I carry you to the bed.
TANYA	You drag me to the couch.
GREG	I gently lay you naked on the silken sheets.
TANYA	You throw me across the room.

GREG   I cover you with sweet, gentle kisses.

TANYA   You tie me to the bed post.

GREG   I tenderly make love to you all night.

TANYA   You ravage me in thirty seconds.

GREG   We lay spent in each other's arms.

TANYA   *(Administers the coup de grace)* You watch "Nightline."

GREG   *(Aware that he's failed for some reason)* I think it would be best all around, if we didn't see each other anymore. *(They haughtily exit in opposite directions...Tanya past the entering Lois and John)*

LOIS   There were other men, John.

JOHN   I understand...A woman alone.

LOIS   While I was married, I mean.

JOHN   From what you told me about your ex...

LOIS   Many other men.

JOHN   We all get lonely.

LOIS   Dozens of other men.

JOHN   Despair does strange things to people.

LOIS   I couldn't get enough.

JOHN   I've experienced my own share of desperation.

LOIS   Young   men...Old   men...Tall   men...Short
            men...Bald   men...Great   hairy   men...Rich
            men...Poor men...

JOHN   Human companionship, even just for a night, is a
            need we all...

LOIS   Taxi drivers...Delivery boys...Upholsterers.

JOHN   Some feel the need more strongly than others.

LOIS   Men of all races, creeds and colors...Sometimes two
            and three at a time.

JOHN   You were crying out in the wilderness.

LOIS   My indiscretions don't bother you?

JOHN   No. Of course not.

LOIS   *(Pissed)* Robert didn't give a shit either. *(Lois strides off leaving a bewildered Johnn behind. He turns to exit, passing Carl who is entering. Carl sits down, looks around and spies Mary who has just entered.)*

CARL   Carl, my man, this could be your lucky night.

MARY   *(Sees Carl eyeing her)* Cute guy.

CARL   Terrific hair.

MARY   Nice shoulders. *(They begin to circle one another in a kind of mating dance.)*

CARL   Sexy.

MARY   Expensive suit.

CARL   Sensational figure.

MARY   A very strong possibility.

CARL   Great legs.

MARY   Probably a college graduate…Vice President of Marketing, maybe.

CARL   Terrific hooters.

MARY   Probably knocks down about seventy…eighty thou a year. *(He crosses over to her)*

MARY   He's coming over.

CARL   Can I buy you a drink?

MARY   *(Trying to sound bored and worldly and not particularly interested)* Sure…Why not? *(A bed slides in. Mary crosses to it)*

CARL   Schoolteacher…I was close. *(He gets into bed.)*

MARY   He seemed taller from a distance. *(Slides into bed next to Carl)*

CARL   She looked thinner with her clothes on.

MARY   Should I tell him what I like?

CARL   Her boobs are smaller than I thought.

MARY   Why bother?

CARL   No way this is a twenty five year old body. *(He nuzzles her)*

MARY   I'd better not get too excited.

CARL   This one's gonna be a real challenge.

MARY   He's probably one of those premature types.

CARL   Christ!!!

MARY   Oh no!!!!!!

CARL   I left my jacket at the cleaners…

MARY   My ceiling's got water stains.

CARL   Damn!

MARY   Oh, just look at him. I know exactly what he's thinking.

CARL   I really wanted to wear that jacket tomorrow.

MARY   (Moans) Oh God!

CARL   Alright!!!

MARY   I've got a cramp in my foot.

CARL   She's really getting turned on.

MARY   Let's hope he's not out to set a world land speed record.

CARL   Come on, honey…

MARY   I hate faking it.

CARL   She's probably the type that likes to go all night.

MARY   I can feel his heart pounding…

CARL   Good think I'm in the best shape of my life.

MARY   I hope he's alright.

CARL   What the hell is she doing now?

MARY   Didn't anybody ever tell him what elbows were for?
            (Mary rolls him over and gets on top)

CARL   She's getting on top...What do you expect from a woman with a minor in women's studies? *(He rolls her onto her back)*

MARY   Eeeuuuwwww...He's drooling.

CARL   Dammit...My hand is stuck in the mattress.

MARY   Oh God...He's an ear licker.

CARL   Easy to see why she lives alone.

MARY   Funny, he never mentioned an ex-wife or anything...

CARL   Probably too busy pursuing a "career."

MARY   I wonder what's wrong with him.

CARL   Shit, my whole leg is asleep.

MARY   Oh, great...He can't sustain. Now we know.

CARL   I can't move. *(A phone rings)*

MARY   Dammit, there's the phone.

CARL   Her phone…Thank God.

MARY   Why didn't I turn on the answering machine?

CARL   She's not going to answer it.

MARY   If I answer it he'll probably get mad. *(After a few rings we hear Mary's phone message.)*

PHONE   "Hi…This is Mary. I'm busy right now and can't come to the phone. But if you'll leave a message I'll get back to you as soon as I can."

CARL   Probably another guy. *(After the beep we hear the sound of a woman's voice.)*

PHONE   "Mary…Mary…Are you there?"

MARY   Oh God…It's my mother.

CARL   I'm losing it.

MARY   Oh God, now I'm losing it.

CARL   I lost it.

MARY   He'll be out the door in five minutes.

CARL   She can't wait for me to leave.

MARY   I've forgotten his name.

CARL   *(Speaks to Mary)* I guess I'd better be going. *(He gets out of bed)*

MARY   I guess.

CARL   I have an early meeting.

MARY   Me too.

CARL   It was really great meeting you Margie.

MARY   Mary.

CARL   Mary…Of course…

MARY   Of course.

CARL   See ya. *(He crosses back into the bar)*

MARY   Right…See ya. *(Mary gets out of bed and crosses back into the bar. Carl spots a woman offstage.)*

CARL	Great hair. *(He exits as Mary spots a man offstage.)*
MARY	Cute buns. *(She exits past Lois and Harold)*
LOIS	Robert criticized me constantly.
HAROLD	For the life of me, I don't see what there is to criticize.
LOIS	I'm not used to being so accepted. Isn't there anything about me you want to change?
HAROLD	How do you improve on perfection?
LOIS	Robert found fault with everything I did.
HAROLD	Robert was a fool.
LOIS	First it was my cooking.
HAROLD	My only complaint is the weight I'm putting on from it.
LOIS	Then it was the way I decorated the house.
HAROLD	Everyone loves what you've done with my place. I hate to leave to go to work in the morning, it's so beautiful.

LOIS   No matter what I did, it was wrong. No matter what I said…He was right and I was wrong.

HAROLD   I find your judgement remarkable…I value your opinion.

LOIS   We fought over everything.

HAROLD   Sometimes a good argument can clear the air.

LOIS   We didn't just argue. We fought. I'm talking knocked down, drag out fights.

HAROLD   How awful for you.

LOIS   Lamp throwing…Vase breaking…Window smashing brawls.

HAROLD   My God.

LOIS   He twisted my arm once when I wouldn't give in to him.

HAROLD   You must have been terrified.

LOIS   I had it in a sling for two weeks.

HAROLD   There are laws against that.

LOIS   I got even, though...I broke his nose with a frozen leg of lamb. There was blood everywhere.

HAROLD   Good for you.

LOIS   Claw, scratch, bite, kick, punch. Some of our battles were monumental.

HAROLD   You mean too much to me for that to ever happen between us.

LOIS   *(Getting orgasmic once again)* And then we'd have sex...Wild, passionate, mind blowing sex. *(Harold gets the picture and slowly exits past Martha who is straightening Larry's tie.)*

MARTHA   Here, let me help you with that.

LARR   Thank you, darling.

MARTHA   Handsome as a prince. Who is it, tonight?

LARRY   Susan. A salesgirl I met while picking out your birthday present.

MARTHA   And a lovely gift it was, too.

LARRY   Susan said you'd like it. She was the one who really selected it. You know how I am with those things.

MARTHA   Thank her for me. She has excellent taste in jewelry...and men.

LARRY   I'll tell her what you said...She'll be pleased to hear it.

MARTHA   Is Susan pretty?

LARRY   Lovely...Almost as lovely as you.

MARTHA   You think Peter will like the way I look?

LARRY   He'll love you.

MARTHA   I hope so. He is such a sexy man.

LARRY   Before you go.

MARTHA   Can it wait, Larry. I am running a little late.

LARRY   This will only take a second.

MARTHA My dearest always comes first. Besides, it's good to keep a man waiting. Gets his juices perking.

LARRY I have a terrible confession to make, Martha.

MARTHA What is it, dear? What's wrong?

LARRY Remember our conversation last year?

MARTHA Which one?

LARRY The one we had after Tony and Judy broke up when she found out about his affair.

MARTHA Yes…That was where we agreed that statistically, we'd be faced with the same problem, sooner or later.

LARRY And we decided that our marriage was much too important for it to flounder on the rocks of infidelity.

MARTHA Poetically said dear. But can you get to the point?

LARRY It's about the agreement we reached to set aside every Tuesday night for each of us to see whoever we wanted openly and above board.

MARTHA So long as it didn't interfere with the marriage.

LARRY   It's about those Tuesday nights.

MARTHA   They are working out wonderfully, too. Aren't they?

LARRY   Yes…Well…That's what I want to talk to you about.

MARTHA   It sounds serious.

LARRY   It is. Quite serious.

MARTHA   Oh dear.

LARRY   It's not what you're thinking.

MARTHA   Then you haven't gotten involved.

LARRY   No.

MARTHA   Good.

LARRY   It's something else.

MARTHA   Go on. Please. I want to help in any way I can.

LARRY   It's about last Tuesday night.

MARTHA   Last Tuesday…You were with someone named Joan, or Joanne, or something like that.

LARRY   That's not quite true.

MARTHA   Whatever her name. As long as you enjoyed yourself.

LARRY   I wasn't with a woman.

MARTHA   Ohmygod!!!!!

LARRY   It's not that Martha.

MARTHA   Then what the hell is it?

LARRY   I was at the movies.

MARTHA   The movies???

LARRY   A double bill. "Dirty Harry" and "Magnum Force"…Clint Eastwood.

MARTHA   Clint Eastwood?

LARRY   It was the same the week before. "Ghostbusters" and "Groundhog Day." They both had Bill Murray in them. He's the fellow from "Saturday Night…"

MARTHA I know where Bill Murray is from. If you couldn't find a date, why didn't you say so? It's no big deal. One or two Tuesday nights?

LARRY It's not that I couldn't find a date. I haven't been looking for one. I've never looked for one. I've been going to the movies every Tuesday night.

MARTHA Every Tuesday night for the last six months?

LARRY It's been awful. You don't realize how much junk Hollywood turns out until…

MARTHA You louse.

LARRY I didn't know how to tell you.

MARTHA What about your secretary?

LARRY I never touched her.

MARTHA Ohmygod. And here I've been making all those little innuendos to her over the phone. What must she think of me?

LARRY She just thinks you're a little brassy.

MARTHA
And I suppose while Kenny and I were at the Marriott you and his wife never...?

LARRY
Never.

MARTHA
How am I ever going to face that woman again? What is wrong with you?

LARRY
I don't know.

MARTHA
We had an agreement.

LARRY
Can you ever forgive me?

MARTHA
All this time I thought you were getting it on with some waitress or the wife of a friend and you were at the movies.

LARRY
I'm sorry.

MARTHA
This is the lowest thing I have ever heard of.

LARRY
I wanted to sleep with someone...Believe me.

MARTHA
I never even suspected. My God, you came home smelling...reeking...of "My Sin" and "Obsession."

LARRY   I keep it in the carl.

MARTHA   And what about all those hickeys.

LARRY   Suction cups.

MARTHA   How could you deceive me like this? Slipping around
             behind my back. Don't all our years of marriage
             count for anything?

LARRY   I'm weak, Martha. You're married to a weak man.

MARTHA   And what about tonight?

LARRY   "Tootsie" and "The Graduate" starring…

MARTHA   And how am I supposed to reach climax on the sixth
             floor of the Hilton, knowing that you're alone in
             some movie theatre watching…? I trusted you, Larry.

LARRY   And I betrayed that trust, Martha. I know that. Believe
             me, I'd do anything to be in bed with my secretary right
             now, just to show you how much I love you.

MARTHA   Prove it.

LARRY   How?

MARTHA   Call her up.

LARRY   Now?

MARTHA   Now.

LARRY   I can't call her up now.

MARTHA   Then I'm afraid there is no hope for our marriage. We might as well call the lawyers.

LARRY   No…Please…Not that.

MARTHA   Then you will call your secretary and have her meet you at the Motel Six. *(She hands him the phone. He dials.)*

LARRY   Claire…This is Mr. Johnnson…I'm fine, dear. How are you? That's good. No, nothing's wrong. Don't worry. Your work is impeccable. That's not why…You're typing? Flawless…Claire…I'm not calling about work. It's something personal…I wonder if you could help me out tonight. That is, if you're not doing anything else…Good…I was wondering if you'd care to meet me, in say, about an hour, for dinner and sex…I know this is short notice, Claire…Well, I've always found you attractive, too. Very attractive…I'm sure you've noticed me glancing at your legs from time to time while you take dictation…I thought so…Sometimes I look out from my office and see you sitting at your desk, with your hair up and I wonder to myself what it would be like to run my lips over your neck. You too? I didn't know...Did I mention the times you put my coffee on my desk and I look down the front of your blouse, catching fleeting glimpses of your soft, white...Thirty minutes? Uh...Yes...Sure. See you then.

(Larry hangs up. Some of Martha's enthusiasm has faded with Larry's growing excitement)

MARTHA   Will you accept my apology?

LARRY   For what?

MARTHA   Doubting you.

LARRY   I gave you plenty of reason.

MARTHA   We have to be more trusting. More forgiving. *(Larry is anxious to get going)*

LARRY   Yeah...Right.

MARTHA   This was a test, Larry. We almost failed it.

LARRY   Almost. Gotta go get ready. Claire is picking me up in thirty minutes.

MARTHA   Secretaries like Claire are hard to find.

LARRY   She's one in a million. *(He starts to hurry out)*

MARTHA   Haven't you forgotten something, dear? *(He can't think what it could be. Martha holds out her arms to him. He crosses to her, gives her a quick kiss on the cheek, then hurries off.)*

LARRY   Give my best to Peter. *(He's gone)*

MARTHA   Give my best to Claire. *(Turns to the audience, mustering all the courage at her disposal.)* I'm the luckiest woman in the world. *(She exits past Potter who is on one knee proposing to Lois.)*

POTTER   I love you Lois…More than any woman I've ever known. You're in my thoughts constantly. I want to marry you. I want the honor of knowing that you are my wife. I want to share a home, a bed and a life with you. I will never lie to you, cheat on you or knowingly make you unhappy in any way. I want more than a lifetime marriage with you. I want a lifetime romance. I'll do everything in my power to make our life exciting, joyful, sexy and rewarding. I want to erase every bad memory you have of Robert, your former husband and replace them with only happy memories of me…What do you have to say that Lois?

LOIS   *(Thinks for a few moments, then speaks with anguish and longing)* Oh God, I miss that sonafabitch.

CURTAIN

"I Can Explain"

(Lights up on a bare stage to find RICHARD, JOANNE, FRAN & BOB weaving and dancing around and sometimes with each another.).

JOANNE   Do you think this is a good idea?

BOB   I don't think this is such a good idea.

RICHARD   I think this is a very good idea.

FRAN   Do you have a better idea?

JOANNE   What if Caroline comes home?

RICHARD   She's working. She won't be home till late. She's never home till late.

BOB   I feel terrible. Jim is my partner and this is tax season.

FRAN   I know. That's what makes it so perfect. We both know exactly where he is.

JOANNE   How can we do this? Caroline is my best friend.

RICHARD   And it's a friendship I've always encouraged. Unbutton your blouse.

BOB   What if he finds out? I've never had a partner I
                    trusted as much as Jim.

FRAN   He speaks very highly of you, too. Unbutton my
                    blouse.

JOANNE   What would Caroline do if she found out?

RICHARD   You're such a caring person. I think that's what
                    attracted me to you in the first place.

JOANNE   Really?

RICHARD   That and your legs.

BOB   Every time I see Jim in the office after I've been to
                    bed with you, I'm racked with this terrible guilt.

FRAN   Oh God, I envy Jim your friendship. Feel me up.

(Jim and Caroline enter from opposites sides of the stage.)

JIM   Fran?

CAROLINE   Richard?

FRAN	Jim?
RICHARD	Caroline?
JIM	Fran!
CAROLINE	Richard!
FRAN	Jim!
RICHARD	Caroline!
JIM	Bob!
CAROLINE	Joanne!
BOB	Jim!
JOANNE	Caroline!

(An embarrassed FRAN, BOB, RICHARD and JOANNE notice the audience for the first time...)

FRAN/BOB/RICHARD/JOANNE   *(Defensively)* I can explain!!! *(They exit explaining away to each other. Elaine strides in past Caroline wearing a very short skirt and very high heels and crosses to Jim..)*

ELAINE   Hi.

JIM   Hi.

(Jack enters and crosses to Caroline)

CAROLINE   I'm in therapy.

JIM   I'm an accountant.

CAROLINE   I'm learning to embrace rejection.

JACK   How are you doing?

CAROLINE   You know what they say…Practice makes perfect.

ELAINE   *(disappointed)* Did you say "accountant?"

JIM   You're disappointed aren't you?

ELAINE   That's O.K. You could always balance my checkbook.

CAROLINE   Would you like to make love?

JACK   Excuse me?

CAROLINE   I'm working on being more assertive.

JIM   What were you hoping I'd be?

ELAINE.   Oh, I don't know…An astronaut…A movie star…The quarterback of the Raiders.

JACK   Didn't Margie tell you?

ELAINE   What were you hoping for?

JIM   Me…Not much…Just your average run of the mill Jewish American nymphomaniac.

ELAINE   Well, at least one of us found what he was looking for.

(The realization slowly hits Jim)

CAROLINE   Didn't Margie tell me wha..? Ohmygod. You're married.

JACK   *(offended)* No…No…Please…I'm gay.

(Caroline is stunned. Jack exits. Meanwhile, Jim and Elaine begin tearing each other's clothes off. Caroline turns to talk to her unseen Shrink. Both Caroline's and Jim's Shrinks only appear as voices.)

CAROLINE   I did what you suggested, Doctor.

CAROLINE'S SHRINK   You took the initiative?

CAROLINE   It was very difficult.

JIM'S SHRINK Jim…Jim…*(insistently)* Jim…*(Jim looks around embarrassed. He tries to extract himself from a very aggressive Elaine who refuses to let go.)*

CAROLINE'S SHRINK   Tell me Caroline…How did you…?

(Caroline is as fascinated watching Jim and Elaine as the rest of us.)

CAROLINE'S SHRINK   Caroline…Caroline..

(Jim finally manages to extricate himself from Elaine and hustle her off stage)

CAROLINE   *(not paying attention)* Yes?

JIM'S SHRINK Jim.. Are you alright?

(Elaine reaches out from offstage and tries to yank Jim back into her grasp. He fights free)

JIM I'm fine…Just give me a minute, will ya? *(He tries to put his clothes back in order)*

CAROLINE'S SHRINK   Caroline.

CAROLINE   Yes.

CAROLINE'S SHRINK   We were talking about Jack.

CAROLINE   Jack? Oh, yes. Jack. He was gay. Did I mention that?

JIM   Talk about aggressive women.

CAROLINE'S SHRINK   Caroline, what did you do when Jack told you he was gay?

CAROLINE   Oh…I apologized.

CAROLINE'S SHRINK   You apologized to Jack for inviting him into your bed?

CAROLINE   Actually, I apologized for everything I could think of, including the Reagan Administration.

JIM   I slept with my ex yesterday.

(Fran, Jim's ex, enters. She turns to Jim to zip up her dress.)

FRAN   I needed to find something out.

JIM   And did you?

FRAN   Did I what?

JIM   Find something out.

FRAN   Oh…Yes.

JIM   Care to let me in on it?

FRAN   Bob and I are getting married.

JIM   Congratulations.

FRAN   I had to see if it was really over between us. *(She starts to exit)*

JIM   And?

FRAN   *(Turns back)* It is. *(She exits.)*

JIM I needed to see if it was really over between us…Fran and me.

JIM'S SHRINK And?

JIM   It is. *(He exits.)*

CAROLINE   Okay, Doctor…Where the hell are all these sensitive men I read about all the time?

CAROLINE'S SHRINK   What about Henry?

CAROLINE   What about him?

CAROLINE'S SHRINK   You said Henry was sensitive. That he wasn't afraid to cry…To show his emotions.

CAROLINE   You're right about that, Doctor. Henry was not afraid to cry. He also wasn't afraid to borrow money, not call for weeks on end and leave with my cuisinart.

CAROLINE'S SHRINK   Okay, then what about Peter?

(Jim comes storming back in)

JIM   What is it with women these days, Doc?

CAROLINE'S SHRINK   Peter was very supportive of your carleer.

JIM   They're all turning into men.

CAROLINE   You bet Peter was supportive of my career. He loved it that I worked. Why not? He never did.

JIM'S SHRINK Do you think you might have a problem with assertive women?

JIM   If a woman wants to have a career that's okay with me.

JIM'S SHRINK Then why did you break it off with Karen?

JIM   You mean the architect…Some architect…Couldn't recognize a kitchen when she was in one.

CAROLINE   Please don't take offense at what I'm going to say, Doctor.

JIM   Can I tell you something, Doc?

JIM'S SHRINK That's what we're here for.

CAROLINE   The thing is…

CAROLINE'S SHRINK   Yes…?

JIM   I'm not sure I want to continue these sessions.

JIM'S SHRINK Oh?

CAROLINE   I'm having seconds thoughts about all this therapy stuff.

CAROLINE'S SHRINK   Money problems?

JIM   I'm beginning to think all this introspection is just a lot of navel gazing.

CAROLINE   It's not the money…I just don't see the point anymore.

JIM   You put all this energy into trying to figure out what's wrong with you…

CAROLINE   And after months of talking and talking and talking…

JIM   You realize that there's nothing wrong with you.

CAROLINE/JIM   It's them.

JIM   You can be the most well balanced…

CAROLINE   Mentally sane…

JIM   Emotionally stable.

CAROLINE   Human being…

JIM   On the face of the earth.

CAROLINE   And you still...

JIM   End up in a dead end relationship...

CAROLINE   With some thumb sucking.

JIM   Self involved...

CAROLINE   Sports addicted...

JIM   Mirror obsessed...

CAROLINE   Egocentric..

JIM   Orgasmically challenged...

CAROLINE   Son of a...

JIM   Bitch. *(Jim and Caroline turn and walk up stage)*

CAROLINE'S SHRINK   She'll come crawling back.

JIM'S SHRINK They always do.

(Jim bumps into an entering Margie. Scott enters and bumps into Caroline.)

JIM　　　　　　*(enthusiastically)* Hi.

CAROLINE　　　*(coyly)* Hi. *(They all turn in different directions. Now Caroline bumps into Jim and Margie bumps into Scott)*

MARGIE　　　　*(sexy)* Hi.

SCOTT　　　　　*(extremely cool)* Hi.

(The characters weave in and around each other introducing themselves. The words are not directed at any particular character)

CAROLINE　　　*(forthrightly)* Caroline.

SCOTT　　　　　*(The macho man)* Scott

JIM　　　　　　*(Happily)* Jim

MARGIE　　　　*(Breathlessly)* Margie.

SCOTT　　　　　Drink?

CAROLINE　　　Lunch?

JIM   Coffee?

MARGIE   *(Invitingly)* I'd love to.

CAROLINE   Oh God, don't let me screw this up.

JIM   I think she likes me.

MARGIE   Just don't be so damn pushy, this time.

SCOTT   Go for it...

CAROLINE   I'm not pushy.

SCOTT   And I mean go for it.

CAROLINE   I'm assertive.

JIM   Women don't go for that stuff, anymore.

CAROLINE   Anyway, men like women who are up front.

SCOTT   They say they don't, but they do.

MARGIE   They say they do, but they don't.

(Caroline crosses to Jim. Margie crosses to Scott. They exit arm in arm.)

CAROLINE   It was amicable.

JIM   We gave it a try.

CAROLINE   I know what you mean.

JIM   It just didn't work out.

CAROLINE   I heard he eventually met someone else.

JIM   We never saw each other again.

CAROLINE   But, look at the up side.

JIM   Up side?

CAROLINE   We met.

(They part reluctantly. Caroline crosses to Margie. Jim walks over to Scott.)

CAROLINE   He's the first man I've been out with who didn't try to hustle me right into bed.

MARGIE   Scott showed me his Porsche.

JIM　　　　　　I took her to a Bergman movie.

SCOTT　　　　　I showed her my Porsche.

MARGIE　　　　Five speed…Convertible…CD changer.

CAROLINE　　　He took me to a Bergman movie.

SCOTT　　　　　Forget marathon sex…This was triathalon sex. We did it on the beach, in the middle of the road and on a bicycle.

MARGIE　　　　He let me drive.

SCOTT　　　　　I was incredible.

CAROLINE　　　When he said Bergman…of course, I thought he was talking about "Casablanca."

SCOTT　　　　　The Seventh Seal? You took her to see The Seventh Seal?

JIM　　　　　　She loved it.

CAROLINE　　　It was so depressing. All that symbolism.

JIM　　　　　　You know how it is with women sometimes?

MARGIE   You get that baby out on the open road and it'll do a hundred and twenty without breaking a sweat?

JIM   You're working your ass off trying to get to know them...

SCOTT   Right...You're telling them what you do, what you like, how much money you make...

CAROLINE   I *think* he said he was a dentist

JIM   And all they do is sit there, not hearing a thing your saying..

CAROLINE   Or was it a doctor?

SCOTT   You can tell they're just waiting for you to take a breath so they can jump in and start talking about themselves.

CAROLINE   Maybe it was a dentist

JIM   But, not this one.

CAROLINE   Oh well...

JIM   She really listened..

SCOTT   I can't believe you took her to a Ingmar Bergman movie?

JIM   Hey, I wanted her to think that I thought she was intelligent…

SCOTT   I have never scored after a Bergman movie. Never.

JIM   *(Ruefully)* Neither have I.

(The four of them begin to weave in and around each other)

JIM   She invited me over for dinner.

CAROLINE   Do you have a recipe for enchiladas?

JIM   Should I tell her enchiladas give me diarrhea?

MARGIE   Why, enchiladas?

CAROLINE   I want him to think I'm worldly.

MARGIE   How's the sex?

CAROLINE   Margie!!

SCOTT   She good in the sack?

JIM   Hey, come on…We're talking about a woman I care about.

SCOTT   Not so good, huh?

(Caroline finds her way into his arms. Margie stands next to Scott. She lights up a cigarette)

JIM   Very good.

CAROLINE   I feel very relaxed with him.

JIM   Okay, she's still a little uptight. But, hey, that's understandable.

CAROLINE   He brought me flowers today. It was so sweet. I cried.

JIM   *(To Caroline)* In the best of all possible worlds, nothing would ever change. Everything would stay just the way it is, right now.

CAROLINE   *(Thinking out loud)* Mrs. Caroline Rosen…Mrs. Caroline Higgins Rosen.

(They exit arm in arm, unable to take their eyes off each other)

SCOTT   This is without a doubt the best relationship I've ever been in.

MARGIE   You poor guy.

SCOTT   No I mean it. We have the perfect relationship

MARGIE   Frightening isn't it?

SCOTT   Two people meet. They're attracted to each other. They get it on. No ties. No remorse. No guilt.

MARGIE   Not much of anything, when you look at it.

SCOTT   Exactly.

(They exit as Caroline and Jim return. They both address their unseen Shrinks)

CAROLINE   He wants me to move in with him, Doctor.

JIM   She wants to move in with me, Doc.

JIM'S SHRINK She said that?

JIM   She didn't have to.

CAROLINE   Well, no…He didn't actually spell it out in so many words.

JIM   I can tell.

CAROLINE   He didn't have to…It's that kind of relationship.

CAROLINE'S SHRINK.   I told you they'd be back.

JIM'S SHRINK   Was there ever any doubt?

JIM   Caroline moved in.

SCOTT   I moved in.

MARGIE   He moved in.

SCOTT   I moved in.

JIM   We did it on the couch.

SCOTT   Margie had her period. We played hearts.

CAROLINE   We did it on the kitchen table.

MARGIE   Check, please.

(The four of them stand and begin weaving in and around one another in a sort of mating dance)

JIM   Hey.

MARGIE   Hey.

SCOTT   How are you?

CAROLINE   Couldn't be better.

JIM   You're looking good.

CAROLINE   Still working out?

MARGIE   It must be this new diet.

SCOTT   Three times a week.

CAROLINE   It shows.

SCOTT   Coffee?

CAROLINE   *(Flirtatiously)*Lunch?

JIM   Drink?

MARGIE   *(Forthrightly)* Dinner.

JIM   We've been living together for eight months. Do you
                believe it?

SCOTT   Margie totaled the Porsche.

CAROLINE   It'll be four months tomorrow since I moved in.

MARGIE   I totaled the Porsche..

(They again weave in and around each other)

JIM   Hey.

MARGIE   Hey.

CAROLINE   What's up?

SCOTT   Lookin' good.

MARGIE   Can't complain.

CAROLINE   Couldn't be better.

JIM   Same-o…Same…o.

MARGIE   It's not like Scott and I took any vows.

JIM   I know exactly what you're talking about.

CAROLINE   I thought things would be different.

SCOTT   Why?

(Jim crosses to Scott. Caroline crosses to Margie.)

JIM   *(Forced enthusiasm)* Great game.

SCOTT   Yeah…

CAROLINE   *(Forced enthusiasm)* Nice movie.

MARGIE   If you like happy endings.

(Caroline and Jim walk downstage to address their Shrinks)

CAROLINE   I thought by this time he'd have asked me to marry
                  him, Doctor.

CAROLINE'S SHRINK   Have you told him this?

JIM   She expects me to marry her, Doc.

CAROLINE   I don't have to.

JIM'S SHRINK   She said that?

JIM   She didn't have to.

JIM/CAROLINE   It's that kind of relationship.

(Jim crosses to Scott. Margie crosses to Caroline.)

CAROLINE   Another fucking hockey game. He went to another fucking hockey game.

MARGIE   Tell me about it.

CAROLINE   That's two this week.

MARGIE   Three.

CAROLINE   Who's counting?

(They begin weaving in and around each other again. Jim and Margie brush against each other surreptitiously. Scott and Caroline briefly touch hands. They part, stop for a moment and glance back at each other)

ENSEMBLE   *(Whispering)* Call me.

(Margie takes Jim's arm. Caroline takes Scott's arm)

MARGIE   I find Bergman's use of symbolism, so, I don't know…

JIM   Symbolic?

MARGIE   Yes.

SCOTT   Wanna see my new Jaguar?

(They stop)

ENSEMBLE   I'll call you.

(They weave in and around each other moaning and groaning and writhing)

MARGIE   Oh…

SCOTT   Oh…

JIM   Oh.

MARGIE   Oh

CAROLINE   Oh God.

SCOTT	Oh God.
JIM	Oh God.
MARGIE	Oh God.
JIM	Yes.
MARGIE	Yes.
CAROLINE	Yes.
SCOTT	Yes.
MARGIE	Yes. Yes.
JIM	Yes. Yes.
CAROLINE	Yes. Yes. Yes…
JIM	Oh, God, you're incredible.
SCOTT	Damn, I'm good.

(They stop)

ENSEMBLE   *(Breathlessly)* Call me.

(They continue)

JIM   These things happen…You can't blame yourself.

MARGIE   Who said I was?

CAROLINE   Committing adultery…That's what we're doing.

SCOTT   Don't be ridiculous. For that to happen one of us
                would have to be married.

(They stop)

ENSEMBLE   Don't call me.

*(This time Jim and Caroline links arms as do Scott and Margie. They look
like two couples out for a stroll.)*

JIM   Good dinner.

MARGIE   Terrific wine.

CAROLINE   Spectacular dessert.

SCOTT   Can I pick 'em or can I pick 'em.

(They stop)

ENSEMBLE   *(Mouthing the words)* Call me.

(They weave)

CAROLINE   Margie's my best friend…She's always been there
             for me.

SCOTT   Now you can always be there for me.

MARGIE   Caroline's still my best friend.

JIM   You think I don't like Caroline?

MARGIE   You're sleeping with me and you still like Caroline?

JIM   Of course…She's a very likable person.

MARGIE   That's sick.

(They stop)

ENSEMBLE   I'll call you.

(They start)

CAROLINE   I've never been the other woman before.

SCOTT   You're kidding.

CAROLINE   It's so sexy.

(They stop)

ENSEMBLE   Call me, dammit.

(They weave)

SCOTT   This is a bad time..

JIM   I'm here with a client.

MARGIE   I can't talk now.

CAROLINE   Later.

(They stop)

ENSEMBLE   I told you never to call me at the office.

(They weave)

JIM'S SHRINK Is there anything wrong?

CAROLINE'S SHRINK   Anything you would like to talk about?

ENSEMBLE   No.

JIM'S SHRINK Are you sure?

JIM   Okay…Okay…I feel like I'm suffocating.

CAROLINE   I can't breathe

MARGIE   Would somebody open a window.

SCOTT   No. I can't think of anything.

BOTH SHRINKS   It's perfectly clear…This sense of claustrophobia
                    is obviously brought on by guilt feelings caused
                    by deep seated…

ENSEMBLE   Oh, fuck off.

(They weave)

SCOTT   Hi honey...

CAROLINE   I'm home.

(Scott gives Margie a little peck...Jim gives Caroline the same)

MARGIE   How was...

JIM   Your day?

SCOTT   I kicked ass.

CAROLINE   It's a jungle out there.

(They stop)

ENSEMBLE   Please, call me.

(They weave again)

CAROLINE   Do you think this is a good idea?

JIM   I wonder if this if this is such a good idea.

RICHARD   I think this is a very good idea.

MARGIE   Do you have a better idea?

(They stop)

ENSEMBLE   Why doesn't he/she call me?

(As they weave in and around each other, the women reach out to one man then the other as the men reach out to first one woman, then the other.)

MARGIE   I can't go on like this.

SCOTT   Margie…Caroline

CAROLINE   I've got to make a choice.

SCOTT   Caroline…Margie.

JIM   This whole thing is giving me migraines.

SCOTT   Margie…Caroline…Caroline…Margie…Is this great or what?

(They stop and speak into phones)

JIM   *(Anxious)* Be there.

MARGIE   *(Desperate)* Please, answer.

CAROLINE   *(Pleading)* Where are you?

SCOTT   *(Checks watch)* If I get that damn machine again...

ENSEMBLE   I can't come to the phone right now, but please leave
                a message after the beep...Beep.

(They weave)

CAROLINE   Do you think this is a good idea?

JIM   I don't think this is such a good idea.

RICHARD   I think this is a very good idea.

MARGIE   Do you have a better idea?

CAROLINE   What if Margie comes home?

SCOTT   She's working. She won't be home till late. She's
                never home till late.

JIM   I feel terrible about this.

CAROLINE	You're such a caring person. Unbutton my blouse.
MARGIE	How can we do this? Caroline is my best friend.
SCOTT	And it's a friendship I've always encouraged. Unbutton your blouse.
JIM	What if he finds out?
CAROLINE	What would Margie do if she found out?
SCOTT	You're such a carling person. I think that's what attracted me to you in the first place.
CAROLINE	Really?
SCOTT	That…and your butt, of course.
JIM	Every time I see Scott after I've been to bed with you, I'm racked with this terrible guilt.
MARGIE	Oh God, I envy Scott your friendship. Feel me up.
SCOTT	You and Margie are such opposites.
JIM	You're so different from Caroline.

SCOTT   You give so much.

JIM   You expect so little.

(Scott kisses Caroline. Jim kisses Margie. While kissing the two couples spot each other.)

JIM   Caroline?

CAROLINE   Margie?

SCOTT   Jim?

MARGIE   Scott?

JIM   Scott?

CAROLINE   Jim?

MARGIE   Caroline?

SCOTT   Margie?

JIM   Caroline!!

CAROLINE   Margie!!

SCOTT   Jim!!

MARGIE   Scott!!

JIM   Scott!!

CAROLINE   Jim!!

MARGIE   Caroline!!

SCOTT   Margie!!

(They all notice the audience)

ENSEMBLE   I can explain!!!

CURTAIN

'You've Got Male"

(A MAN ENTERS and walks to the edge of a bare stage.)

MAN: Good evening…At this point in the proceedings I was scheduled to perform for you, still another monologue about the male experience. I'm sorry to say, I won't be doing that. I know you're disappointed and well you should be. I would have been magnificent. However, because I have so much respect for you as an audience and as wonderful human beings and because I care so much about this magnificent institution I call "theatre," I would like to offer you an explanation, if I may.

A few months ago that annoying little person who lives inside my computer announced that I had mail. What it failed to reveal, however, was that the communication was from someone who thought I was idiot enough to believe that for a small investment on my part, I could earn ten thousand dollars a month without getting out of bed.

So, after putting the delete key to the use for which it was designed, I was then told another e-mail had arrived. This time from this very theatre *(Note: You may substitute the name of your theatre here)* which was trolling the internet seeking monologues on the male experience..

"What the hell?" I mused. I was male…I had experience…How hard could it be? But then again it was the *(Insert name of your theatre here)* and I had submitted material to them before. Material to which they had responded with such phrases as "Lacks structure and cohesiveness," as though structure and cohesiveness were some kind of dramatic virtues. "Rambles," was another comment. "Doesn't stick to the point. Never actually makes a point."

They just didn't get it. The fact that my plays don't have a point is exactly the point. *(His anger rising)* If they had looked beyond their own narrow little existences they'd see there is no point in life or anywhere else. Life is pointless. Life rambles from subject to subject, with no beginning and no ending. Life is a tale told by an idiot, full of sound and fury, signifying nothing.

(Impressed with what's just come out of his own mouth)

Wow…That's good. That's very good. I'd better write that down before I forget it. *(Takes out a paper and pencil. He speaks as he writes)* "Life…is like a box of chocolates. You never know what you're going to get." *(Puts away the paper and pencil)*

I'm sorry…Where was I? Oh yes, writing about the male experience…In spite of this theatre's philistine approach to good drama, I decided to press on. I began like I always do by free associating…Letting the subconscious flow unhindered by any real thought. I asked myself what's the first thing you think about when you think about the male experience...Exactly...The female experience.

Women, I pondered...Ah yes...Women... Women ...Women...I let the word roll around on my tongue savoring the sweet, succulent taste that quickly turned bitter and astringent. Women, I muttered... Women...Pain....Pain and loneliness...Women and pain and loneliness. Loneliness, pain and women... Pain, loneliness, women...rejection. Loneliness, pain, women, rejection...Writing. Pain, women, loneliness, rejection, writing...plays. That was it. The old subconscious came through again. If there was one thing with which I had experience up the wazoo it was rejection writing plays.

I had my subject and it had only taken me two minutes tops...Sixty seconds later I had my title... Writing Plays, One Male's Experience With Pain, Loneliness And Rejection...by...By who? I knew I couldn't use my real name. They'd recognize it. Besides they seemed to be unusually alert since the law suit.

I intended for my piece to be seasoned with irony, salted with humor and peppered with innuendo. I needed a name de pen that spelled funny. "What spells funny?", I asked myself and quickly came up with the answer. F...U...N...N...Y spells funny. I played with various versions. Using funny as a first name then as a last...Eventually I dropped the whole idea as too on the schnoz as they say around the Dramatist's Guild and settled on an obscure Greek name. One I had come across in Bartlett's Quotations. I decided to call myself...Anonymous. I knew the guy couldn't take me to court. He was dead and "dead men don't sue."

(Stops and contemplates what he's just uttered) That's good...That's very good. "Dead Men Don't Sue." I hadn't finished this play and I already had a title for my next one. I was on a roll. I poured myself a double scotch and pushed on. All I really needed was a little structure, some conflict, a few lines of dialogue and the money would start rolling in. I drained the glass and started writing.

The way I saw it, the stage lights would come up on a male...Then I thought. That's not enough. No...The lights should come up on an experienced male...No...On a pained, lonely and rejected male. Sets up the character...Lets the audience know what to expect. If I had gone through the first stages of the creative process like a man possessed, I charged into the script itself like a man re-possessed.

His name was going to be...It had to be the right name...A name says a lot about a character. It paints a picture of him…I needed a name that painted a picture of pain, loneliness and rejection. I turned my subconscious loose once again. Gene. Eugene. Greg. Neil. Benji. Floyd. I ran the gamut of emotionally dynamic male monikers. Then it hit me right between the eyes like a brick thrown from close range at a man who was becoming tiresome and annoying…"This is a monologue," I whispered to myself, in case someone was eavesdropping. One character. No one else is there to say his name. He doesn't need a name…He doesn't have a name. He's the character with no name…If that doesn't say pain, loneliness and rejection, my name isn't…Isn't…Well, that's unimportant.

The man with no name speaks. No. Not yet, I reflected…First he looks up at the audience…No, that's too fast…I need to establish some mystery here. Who is this guy? Why doesn't he have a name? Why does he look so pained, lonely and rejected?

I began to re-write. I was already in second draft. This thing was taking on a life of its own. The man with no name enters and walks to center stage. He enters and ambles to center stage…He enters and skips to center stage…He enters and shuffles to center stage…Shuffles…Good, I said aloud, scaring the cat.

But, why "center" stage? His movements can't be arbitrary. Everything in a play needs to be specific...Grounded. Why *does* he ramble to center stage? Why not stage left or stage right? Whoever said "writing was hard" must have been wrestling with stage directions.

I decided not to let important questions bog me down. I knew I could always revisit the stage right, stage left question later. Besides, the dialogue would probably tell me where he goes anyway.

Wherever the hell he is, he looks up at the audience and...Does he have to look up? What if he kept his head down and didn't look at the audience, at all? Hell, he could turn away completely. Just stand there with his back to the audience. I was on to something new. The man with no name backs onto the stage and speaks...

Or *does* he? What if he didn't speak? I mumbled. What if he says nothing? Talk about loneliness, pain and rejection. Why *tell* the audience about pain, loneliness and rejection when I can make you experience it first hand. Make you feel what's its like to be rejected over and over and over and over and over....*(Pulls himself together)*

Well, isn't that what theatre's supposed to be? A shared experience? "Of course." I caterwauled. "I'll give those sonsabitches an experience they'll never forget." Nothing personal, you understand…That's just how writers talk.

"Okay," I coughed. "He enters" Why? Why does he enter? What's his motivation for entering? If he's lonely, in pain and feeling rejected, why does even bother entering? Why doesn't he just stay where the hell he is? Why subject himself to even more pain and humiliation in front of a group of people, half of whom are probably women…Just like the women who have taunted, teased and rejected him time after time after time after time. Women, with their perfume and jewelry and high heels and long legs and sweet, succulent…

Then it hit me like a ton of bricks falling on a man who had long ago overstayed his welcome. "That's it," I sneeezed.. "The bastard never enters". He rejects the audience completely. He rejects the very idea of the audience just the way it's rejected him. It was the most revolutionary idea to hit the theatre since the five dollar decaffeinated coffee. The bastard never enters. Let's see Beckett top that.

I was beside myself with glee. Suddenly, the solution I was looking for was staring me right in the face like a demented stranger on the subway who's just escaped from a mental ward and thinks you're his long lost mother. No longer, did I have to worry whether the character hopped, rolled or sashayed. It no longer mattered whether he was center stage, stage left or stage right or faced the audience or turned his back to it. But, best of all, it solved the one problem that has dogged every writer down through history...Words. I no longer needed any. I went back to work with a renewed lease on life. My previous lease having expired for lack of funding. "He," I started to peck when it hit me like a piano dropped from a ten story window onto a man whose behaviour had become tedious and self-serving. "Who says he has to be a he?" This theatre? Who the hell is this theatre to tell me what gender my character has to be? I'm a writer, by God. An artist and no one tells me what to write.

I returned to my computer with the Windows 98 upgrade, read the fatal error message, re-booted and began to type. "Dear *(enter name of your theatre),*" I lied. I read with total ambivalence your e-mail seeking monologues about the male experience. Well, thanks but no thanks. While lesser beings may kowtow to your dictatorial demands...as an artist I reserve the right not to write what I choose not to write and whom I choose not to write it for."

It was a difficult choice but one I knew I had to make in defense of my art and the art of writers everywhere. Do I need this goddam theatre? The answer is a resounding "No." Do I need the approval of audiences that do not understand my art? Again..."No'. Do I need the attention and approval of the half of you out there who have the balls to call yourselves "women?" "No, no a thousand times no."

(Stops and thinks) That's good....That's very good. I've got to remember that....Where was I? Oh yeah...*(Picks up his tirade where he left off)* No...I do not need your understanding or approval. "Why not?," you may ask...I'll tell you why not. Because I have talent...Because I have integrity. But, mostly, because I can earn ten thousand dollars a month without even getting out of bed. *(He wheels and exits)*.

CURTAIN

"*Cracking The Whip*"

Setting: Inside the confused mind of Alan Bedford

Characters:

ALAN BEDFORD—late thirties…confused.

SUSAN—Alan's fiancee—thirty and prim

AMBER—early twenties, pretty, sexy and wearing next to nothing.

LAURA—mid thirties, large breasted, dressed in black s&m boots with whip and outfit to match

(Lights up on all the characters arrayed on stage. Susan can not see Amber or Laura. Amber can not see Susan or Laura. Laura sees everything. Alan sees what he wants to see. Agitated, Alan crosses to Laura.)

ALAN	You can go. You're not needed here.
LAURA	It's your mind, Alan. All you have to do is stop thinking about me and I'm out of here.
ALAN	Trust me, I'd like nothing better than to not think of you.
LAURA	*(To audience)* Alan is in crisis.
ALAN	I'm not in crisis…Just a little tired.

LAURA   *(To audience)* Alan couldn't rise to the occasion last
                 night.

ALAN   Go ahead...Tell the whole world...Call Peter
                 Jennings, why don't you?

LAURA   You never had a hydraulic problem with me.

ALAN   I didn't dare.

SUSAN   It's okay, Alan... Really... There's nothing for you to
                 be embarrassed about...These things happen.

ALAN   Maybe to you. Not to me.

SUSAN   What's that supposed to mean? Maybe to you, not
                 to me.

ALAN   Nothing...Nothing...I didn't mean anything.

SUSAN   Are you saying this is my fault?

ALAN   No...No...It's nobody's fault.

SUSAN   Maybe you should think about seeing a doctor.

ALAN   I am a doctor.

SUSAN	No, you're not…You're a dentist.
ALAN	*(To audience)* Is it any wonder dentists have the highest suicide rate of any profession?
LAURA	Is that supposed to be some kind of ploy for sympathy?
ALAN	From you?…That's a laugh. No. I was just pointing out a little known fact.
LAURA	Your life story. A collection of little known facts.
SUSAN	I'm only concerned for your sake.
ALAN	*(To Laura)* See…A woman concerned for my welfare. Listen and learn. *(to Susan)* I'm fine.
SUSAN	I know how something like this can damage a man's self esteem.
ALAN	My self-esteem will be up and around in no time.
SUSAN	It is me, isn't it?
ALAN	It's not you.
SUSAN	I don't excite you anymore.

ALAN   This has nothing to do with you.

SUSAN   You've never had this problem before, have you?

ALAN   No, I've never had this problem before.

SUSAN   Then why now?

LAURA   Alan…You know, of course, that impotence is usually
                a symptom of unresolved conflict.

ALAN   I'm not impotent.

SUSAN   I didn't say you were impotent.

ALAN   Could we just drop the subject?

(Amber crosses to Alan, drapes herself all over him and speaks in a gooey kind of sexiness)

AMBER   Alan…Honey…

ALAN   *(Goes into baby talk mode)* Yes, sweetie, baby.

LAURA   A warning to the first three rows. I may hurl at any
                moment.

AMBER	How do you, like, feel?
ALAN	Finey winey…I feel absolutely finey winey.
AMBER	But, do, y'know…feel like wonderful?
ALAN	I just said I did.
AMBER	No. You said you felt finey winey.
ALAN	Well, I meant wonderful.
AMBER	But you feel wonderful a lot, don't you?
ALAN	No, I wouldn't say a lot.
AMBER	Like how much?
ALAN	Some.
AMBER	So this isn't some kind of like new experience for you.
ALAN	No.
LAURA	But I'd say this conversation is.

AMBER   I feel like really good, y'know?

ALAN   Oh, I know.

AMBER   And I don't, y'know...feel like bad about it.

LAURA   You might want to explain to her that one usually cancels out the other.

AMBER   Y'see feeling good always makes me feel like totally bummed. I mean every time I feel happy, I begin to like think about all the people around the world y'know who aren't happy and then I feel like guilty and then I get like all depressed, y'know.

ALAN   But you're not depressed now?

AMBER   Oh, no.

LAURA   Then how does she know she's happy?

ALAN   Will you butt out...*(To Amber)* You were actually expecting to feel bad.

AMBER   Well, like, yeah.

ALAN   But, why, dumpling?

AMBER   Because I had all those y'know…orgasms last night
               and I keep thinking about all the women around the
               world waking up this morning who had like only one
               or two.

LAURA   *(to Alan)* You're making this up aren't you?

ALAN   God, you're incredible…(*He puts his arms around
               Amber and begins to rub*) Have I mentioned your
               thighs in the last five minutes?

SUSAN   *(horrified)* My thighs? I knew it. You think I'm get-
               ting fat.

ALAN   I don't think you're getting fat.

SUSAN   Then why are you fixating on my thighs?

ALAN   I'm not fixating…I wasn't even…

SUSAN   Even what?

ALAN   Nothing.

LAURA   Does…uh…*(Indicates Amber)*…?

ALAN   Amber…Her name is Amber.

LAURA   Amber...Of course...Does Amber know she's just a...?

ALAN   *(Quickly cutting in)* Memory...Memory...Just like you...Only, she's a good memory. A pleasant memory. A memory I remember fondly.

AMBER   You wanna like...y'know...Do it again?

ALAN   Oh boy...Do I.

AMBER   Last night was like the best sex I ever had.

LAURA   Have you ever considered fiction writing as an alternate career?

ALAN   I could make love to you forever.

SUSAN   You just said you were tired.

LAURA   You are a bundle of contradictions, aren't you? One minute you can't light the old fire, and the next you're a late blooming nymphomaniac.

ALAN   For your information only women are nymphomaniacs.

LAURA   Another piece of sexist propaganda.

ALAN   Men are "satyrs."

LAURA   Oh, sure…Women are maniacs while men are char-
            acters from Greek mythology.

ALAN   *(To Amber)* Am I really the best lover you've ever had?

SUSAN   I thought we agreed not to delve into each other's past.

ALAN   Because you're the best I've ever had.

SUSAN   *(Pleased)* Really?

LAURA   The best?

ALAN   Yes, the best.

LAURA   *(Cracks her whip)* The best?

ALAN   *(Nervously)* Okay…Maybe the second best.

LAURA   That's better.

SUSAN   If you really feel that I'm…Maybe we could give it
            another…

AMBER   You're like the hottest dude I've ever done.

ALAN   Tell me about it.

LAURA   Hey, "dude" Fantasy is one thing…Mental illness is
               another.

ALAN   You just can't stand the fact that I'm happy, can you?

LAURA   Happy? You're hallucinating.

ALAN   Isn't that the clinical definition of happy?

LAURA   You're a very sick man. You know that, don't you?

ALAN   And you know you're free to go anytime.

LAURA   And you know I can't do that, until you stop thinking
               about me. And that raises another question…Why
               are you thinking about me?

ALAN   Maybe I like watching you squirm.

LAURA   You think I'm jealous?

ALAN   You are, aren't you?

LAURA   No.

ALAN   Of course you are.

LAURA   If I am, it's only because you want to think I am.

ALAN   Hey, that's good enough for me. *(He puts his arms around Susan and Amber)*

LAURA   Don't push me Alan.

ALAN   Why not?

LAURA   Just don't do it.

ALAN   You can't threaten me. I'm in control here…Not you…Me…This is my mind we're in. If I want two women to be in love with me, I only have to think it. If I want you to be jealous, I just think it and you're jealous. And if I want you to stand there and watch me make love to two women who are younger and prettier than you, then you're going to stand there and…

LAURA   *(To Susan and Amber)* Girls.

ALAN   What are you doing?

LAURA   Can I have your attention please?

ALAN   It won't work. They don't know you're here.

LAURA   There's something both of you need to know.

ALAN   You're wasting your time.

SUSAN   *(To Laura)* Who are you?

LAURA   We'll get to that in a minute.

SUSAN   *(To Alan)* Who is she?

ALAN   Who?

SUSAN   *(Points to Laura)* Her…*(Disgustedly)* This.

ALAN   There's no one there. Are you feeling alright? Maybe if you lied down.

AMBER   Alan, who are these people?

ALAN   What people?

AMBER   *(Indicates Susan)* Well, like her and like her.

SUSAN   I'm Susan...Alan's fiancee.

AMBER   *(Stunned)* Fiancee?

ALAN   *(To Laura)* Stop this right now.

AMBER   You're engaged?

SUSAN   The wedding's in a month...Who may I ask are you?

AMBER   You never said anything about getting married.

LAURA   Shame on you Alan.

SUSAN   Alan, who is this woman?

ALAN   What woman? I don't see any woman.

LAURA   It won't work Alan. The cat's...like...out of the bag.

SUSAN   *(To Amber)* And just what is your relation to my fiancee?

AMBER   Let's just say I'm the woman he's given more climaxes than a Stephen King novel.

LAURA   *(To Alan)* Delusional doesn't even come close to describing your state of mind.

SUSAN   *(Astonished)* You're having an affair!

ALAN   I'm not having an affair…

AMBER   You had sex with her. She just said so.

ALAN   Okay…But only up here in my mind.

SUSAN   Is that supposed to make me feel better?

AMBER   What do you mean, only up here in your mind?

LAURA   Maybe, I can explain.

ALAN   You stay out of this.

SUSAN   And did you sleep with her too?

LAURA   Many times. Many times.

SUSAN   Right…But only up here in your mind.

LAURA   No...Never in his mind...At least, not that I'm aware of.

AMBER   Will someone explain what's going on?

LAURA   (To Amber) Sure...Your boyfriend, here, has just a teensy weensy little problem with reality.

AMBER   What does that mean?

LAURA   Take you for instance.

AMBER   Me?

LAURA   You and Alan get along well don't you.

AMBER   Yeah...Sure...He's the best...

LAURA   I think we've covered that. The reason that you and Alan get along so well is because, well, frankly... you're not real.

AMBER   Of course, I'm real.

LAURA   I know this is difficult to understand, but, trust me...you don't really exist.

AMBER   Of course I exist.

LAURA   No…You don't. You never have.

AMBER   Alan, tell her to stop saying that. Tell her it's not true.

ALAN   I can't.

AMBER   I'm confused.

LAURA   A relationship with Alan will do that to you.

AMBER   How can I not exist?

LAURA   You're a fantasy.

AMBER   A fantasy?

LAURA   You're a figment of Alan's imagination. Girls like you don't really exist except in the fevered minds of middle aged men like the Big Kahuna here.

ALAN   Don't listen to her…She likes to make me miserable. That's why she married me…That's also why she divorced me.

SUSAN   You were married to her?

LAURA	Nice to meet you…I'm Laura Bedford. In real life I'm a much nicer woman with much smaller breasts. But this is how Alan likes to think of me. *(sizes Susan up)* And I guess this is how he likes to think of you.
SUSAN	I don't like the tone of that remak?
LAURA	You can't really be this much of a tight ass in reality. No one can.
SUSAN	I beg your pardon.
LAURA	Sorry…I'm sure you're a very lovely, caring woman. But Alan has a habit of recreating the women in his life to suit his own purposes.
SUSAN	Is she right, Alan? Do you really think of me as a…a….
LAURA	Tight…Ass…It's okay, you can say it.
AMBER	Is it true, Alan? What she said…I don't really exist? I'm like a fantasy?
ALAN	You do exist…In my mind you exist. You're my fantasy…That has to count for something.

SUSAN   I can't believe this. You're getting married in a
               month. Men who are getting married in a month are
               not supposed to be having fantasies about..
               about…"hussies."

LAURA   Hussies? What is the Roaring Twenties?

AMBER   What did she just call me?

LAURA   A hussy. It's anal retentive for tramp, bimbo, slut…

AMBER   *(Advances on Susan)* Who are you calling a slut,
               you…*(Looks to Laura for the word)*

LAURA   Ball buster?

SUSAN   *(To Amber)* How dare you call me a…a…

LAURA   Come on, Susie…You can say it…Ball buster.

*(Susan lunges at Amber. Alan tries to separate them and takes and elbow in
the stomach that drops him to his knees. Susan and Amber get into a knock
down, drag out fight)*

LAURA   Alan, I think we all understand the symbolism of
               what's going on here…The inner conflict. The strug-
               gle between responsibility and escape…But don't you
               think you're carrying it a little too far? If you don't

stop this, it could do permanent damage to your psyche, not to mention a few internal organs.

(Alan, still in pain, struggles to his feet…He tries to break up the fight without getting sucker punched again.)

ALAN   Susan…Amber…

(He ducks as a punch sails by his ear…He finally grabs Susan around the waist and lifts her in the air and pulls her away, still punching and kicking)

ALAN   Behave yourselves…Both of you.

(He puts Susan down.)

ALAN   You oughta be ashamed of yourselves…Carrying on like this.

LAURA   Take it from me, ladies…he's not worth it.

ALAN   Now, listen to me…All of you. I want you all to go away. I'm going to close my eyes and when I open them you'll all be gone. *(Closes his eyes…When he opens them, the three women are still there, arms folded, waiting for an explanation.)*

ALAN   Will you all please go away.

LAURA   Stop thinking of us.

ALAN   I'm trying.

LAURA   Try harder. *(He closes his eyes again. When he opens them, the women are still there)*

ALAN   I'm haunted.

LAURA   You're troubled.

ALAN   I'm not troubled.

LAURA   You're very troubled…That's why you can't get rid of us. You're filled with doubt and remorse and guilt and whole bunch of other wonderful things that allow me to make your life a living hell.

ALAN   There's nothing wrong with me that a good night's sleep won't cure.

LAURA   Alan, you can lie to us all you want. We're just figments of your warped imagination. But, you are completely incapable of lying to yourself. It's a very endearing quality, actually. And, one I might add, that makes it so easy to torture you. Susan…You were right when you guessed that Alan was having second thoughts.

SUSAN I never said Alan was having second thoughts. I said men who are getting married in a month don't have fantasies about...*(Can't bring herself to say the word)*

(Amber starts to move on Susan. Alan holds her back)

LAURA What the hell do you think those fantasies are, if not second thoughts?

SUSAN It's all her fault...The little tramp.

(Amber lunges at Susan and the fight starts all over again)

(Alan throws up his hands in resignation and walks downstage. The lights on Susan and Amber fade)

ALAN *(To Laura)* Do you remember the day I asked you to marry me?

LAURA You never asked me to marry you.

ALAN Of course, I did? It was on a Tuesday.

LAURA You never asked me to marry you.

ALAN Then why do I still have alimony payments?

LAURA   Because I asked you for a divorce.

ALAN   Okay.

LAURA   Okay, what?

ALAN   Proves my point.

LAURA   What point?

ALAN   That I asked you to marry me.

LAURA   It doesn't prove anything.

ALAN   If I didn't ask, you couldn't answer.

LAURA   So?

ALAN   And if you didn't answer then we would never have
               gotten married.

LAURA   What's your point?

ALAN   We're divorced.

LAURA   I know that.

ALAN   Which means we were once married which means I asked you to marry me.

LAURA   You never asked me to marry you Alan.

ALAN   Didn't we just cover this?

LAURA   You left out a ring where I would find it.

ALAN   Okay.

LAURA   And when I asked you if you were asking me to marry you…

ALAN   Yeah?

LAURA   You asked me what I would say if you were asking me. You never asked me to marry you Alan…You simply tested the waters.

ALAN   Why did you divorce me?

LAURA   Is that why you dredged me up from the recesses of this cluttered attic you call a mind?

ALAN   I need to know.

LAURA   I told you.

ALAN   You said you needed space…To find yourself.

LAURA   I typed you out a three page list, single spaced.

ALAN   I don't remember that.

LAURA   That's because you only remember what you want to
               remember.

ALAN   You think that's true?

LAURA   Alan why am I here?

ALAN   You think I only remember what I want to remember?

LAURA   I don't know Alan. I only think what you think.

ALAN   You've always had a mind of your own.

LAURA   And now I have a mind of your own.

ALAN   Just because you're not flesh and blood, doesn't mean
               you can't think for yourself.

LAURA	I'm a fiction, Alan...Fiction's don't have minds. They're only extensions.
ALAN	I give you complete freedom to think anyway you want to.
LAURA	It doesn't work that way.
ALAN	What if I say it does? You're my fiction.
LAURA	Exactly.
ALAN	Here you are.
LAURA	Oh yes, here I am.
ALAN	Arguing with me...Disagreeing with me. If that isn't a mind of your own.
LAURA	I'm sure I'm only doing it because you want me to do it.
ALAN	That's my point.
LAURA	I'm only disagreeing because you want me to disagree. If you wanted me to tell you the moon and stars set over your shoulder, I'd probably be doing that.

ALAN   Every conscience has a mind of its own. That's the nature of a conscience.

LAURA   Is that what you think I am? Your conscience?

ALAN   What else would you be?

LAURA   Well, if I am your conscience then I must be one of those early twenty first century types that doesn't like to get involved.

ALAN   Of course you're my conscience…You annoy me…You plague me…You nag me.

LAURA   I never nagged you.

ALAN   You always complained I was too conservative… Too careful.

LAURA   That wasn't nagging. That was simply pointing out the obvious.

ALAN   I'm beginning to think you were right.

LAURA   Really?

ALAN   Really. Feel better?

LAURA	I don't feel anything, actually. It's one of the benefits of being a delusion.
ALAN	You're not a delusion.
LAURA	Then what am I? And don't say your conscience again. I'm not buying that.
ALAN	You're a manisfestation.
LAURA	I see…Of what? A manisfestation of what?
ALAN	The part of me that knows the truth.
LAURA	Your version of the truth. Look at you, Alan. You're so internalized you can only hold arguments with yourself.
ALAN	Don't you understand why you're resisting?
LAURA	Because I don't want to be here. Can you understand that?
ALAN	The reason you don't want to be here is because I'm trying to suppress the part of me you represent.
LAURA	Then suppress…Please suppress.

ALAN   I can't...Anymore. That's my problem.

LAURA   Well, then work on that problem...With help and
              counseling you could learn to eliminate, altogether,
              that part of your personality I represent. Think how
              easy things would be if you could just drift through
              life completely unaware of yourself. Imagine how
              much you could accomplish if you didn't have to ago-
              nize over the consequences.

ALAN   I recognize I have a few shortcomings.

LAURA   I could have told you that.

ALAN   Where do you think I learned it?

LAURA   Do you enjoy punishing yourself like this?

ALAN   No, of course not.

LAURA   Then dismiss me from you mind.

ALAN   No pain, no gain.

LAURA   Alan please find yourself another manifestation.

ALAN   Every one has a conscience whether they want to admit or not. I'm just willing to embrace mine. *(Starts to hug her)*

LAURA   Don't embrace me.

ALAN   *(Backs away)* Sorry. You always told me I should act more on impulse. I'd find life more enjoyable.

LAURA   That was then.

ALAN   I followed your advice.

LAURA   Good…Are you enjoying life more?

ALAN   I don't know when I've been more miserable.

LAURA   I'm sorry. I guess being fully alive doesn't work for everybody.

ALAN   I led with my heart when I should've led with my mind. And now I'm in trouble.

LAURA   This is your attempt to lay a guilt trip on me, isn't it. You're saying I'm responsible for your problem and now I have to help you resolve it.

ALAN   I'm only stating the facts. If you choose to interpret it...

LAURA   Well, this should make one helluva headline. Man lays guilt trip on own conscience.

ALAN   If I can't turn to my conscience, who can I turn to?

LAURA   Call your shrink.

ALAN   She doesn't understand me.

LAURA   Then talk to the real Laura.

ALAN   She wouldn't give me the sweat off her brow if I was drowning.

LAURA   Hey...You're talking about someone I share...What do I share with her?

ALAN   An annoying habit of being right. Otherwise, not much.

LAURA   You don't want to marry Susan, do you?

ALAN   I don't know. You have all the answers.

LAURA   I just have questions. Can I go now?

ALAN   Help me or I won't stop thinking of you.

LAURA   That's blackmail.

ALAN   I'm a desperate man. If I have to blackmail my con-
            science into helping me, I'll do it.

LAURA   I am not your conscience. Stop calling me that. At
            best I'm a neuroses. What other answer is there? I
            mean, a healthy person does not conjure up the
            image of his ex-wife to help him solve his problems.

ALAN   I'm unorthodox.

LAURA   That's not the first word that comes to mind when
            someone thinks about Alan Bedford.

ALAN   That's only because they don't know me.

LAURA   No one knows you Alan. You don't know you. I don't
            want to do this Alan.

ALAN   Of course you don't, because I don't want to do this.
            You're just manifesting what I am feeling. I'd rather
            just hide out. Forget what happened.

LAURA   That's what I'd recommend. Take the easy way out.

ALAN   I can't. Not this time.

LAURA   Why do I have the feeling it's not up to me?

ALAN   I suppose if you turn me down it means I'm taking
                the easy way out.

LAURA   It was difficult living with you as your wife. It's
                impossible as...

ALAN   My conscience?

LAURA   I'm out of here.

ALAN   Where are you going?

LAURA   You don't need me anymore.

ALAN   You can't go...I still haven't resolved anything. You're
                the only one I can talk to.

LAURA   Boy, you're more fucked up than I thought you were.

ALAN   What am I going to do?

LAURA	If as you say…I'm your conscience…Then my job is not to provide answers. It's only to annoy the shit out of you.
ALAN	Fine…Go…
LAURA	Do you love Susan?
ALAN	I don't know…What difference does it make? I once loved you.
LAURA	In your own neurotic way, I suppose you did.
ALAN	And look where it got me.
LAURA	Life is choices, Alan.
ALAN	I know. To be or not to be. *(Alan turns upstage. The lights come up on the battling Susan and Amber)* Look at them.
LAURA	What's it going to be?
ALAN	God, I hate reality. It makes so many demands on you.

(The lights fade on Susan and Amber)

LAURA   Then go with Amber.

ALAN   How can I? She's a fantasy.

LAURA   She thinks you're the hottest stud in seven states.

ALAN   You think it's possible to have a really meaningful relationship with a complete fabrication?

LAURA   If anyone can, it's you.

ALAN   Tell me what to do.

LAURA   The right thing.

ALAN   You're no help.

LAURA   Can I go now?

ALAN   Do you have to?

LAURA   I think so.

(She starts to go)

ALAN   You know you're the only woman I ever really loved.

LAURA   Really?

ALAN   No.

LAURA   Good, honest answer.

ALAN   *(Surprised)* That was a good, honest answer…wasn't it? *(Proudly)* How about that. I must be making progress.

LAURA   You must be. You've already moved up one step on the self-esteem ladder.

ALAN   What if we gave it another shot? You and me. What do you say?

LAURA   You'd still be running away from reality.

ALAN   Is that such a bad thing? Reality is highly over rated as far as I'm concerned.

LAURA   Not being real myself, I wouldn't know.

ALAN   But, you do know that if I wanted us to get back together, all I'd have to do is think it. *(Laura cracks her whip. Alan backs away)* Okay…Okay…It was just a thought…Sometimes you can be a real bitch.

LAURA   Isn't that the clinical definition of a conscience? Goodbye, Alan.

ALAN   Will I see you again?

LAURA   Count on it.

(Laura exits. Alan watches her go then turns and walks upstage. The lights come up on Susan and Amber who are still fighting. Alan looks from one to the other and back again, trying to decide, as the lights fade)

CURTAIN

Printed in the United Kingdom
by Lightning Source UK Ltd.
105499UKS00001B/187

9 780595 148936